Getting Around Our City

Linc Jamison

ROSEN
COMMON CORE
READERS

Rosen
Classroom™

New York

Published in 2013 by The Rosen Publishing Group, Inc.
29 East 21st Street, New York, NY 10010

Book Design: Michael Harmon

Photo Credits: Cover Grant Faint/The Image Bank/Getty Images; p. 4 Adisa/Shutterstock.com; pp. 5, 11 Monkey
Business Images/Shutterstock.com; pp. 6, 7 © iStockphoto.com/asiseeit; p. 8 Losevsky Pavel/Shutterstock.com;
p. 9 © iStockphoto.com/BlueOrange Studio; p. 10 Elena Elisseeva/Shutterstock.com; p. 12 © iStockphoto.com/
aabejon; p. 13 Image Source/Image Source/Getty Images; p. 14 Dmitriy Shironosov/Shutterstock.com;
p. 16 (taxi) Maggie 1/Shutterstock.com.

ISBN: 978-1-4488-8722-4
6-pack ISBN: 978-1-4488-8723-1

Manufactured in the United States of America

CPSIA Compliance Information: Batch #WS12RC: For further information contact Rosen Publishing, New York, New York at 1-800-237-9932.

Word Count: 100

Contents

There are many ways
to get around our city.

My friends and I walk to school.

Mike rides the bus to school.

Brian and Carrie ride the bus
to school, too.

Sam rides the subway to the zoo.

Sean and Kim ride the subway
to the zoo, too.

Molly rides her bike to the park.

Dan and Jake ride their bikes
to the park, too.

Leah and Max take a taxi
to their uncle's house.

Laura takes a taxi
to her grandmother's house.

There are many ways
to get around our city.
How do you get around where you live?

City Travel

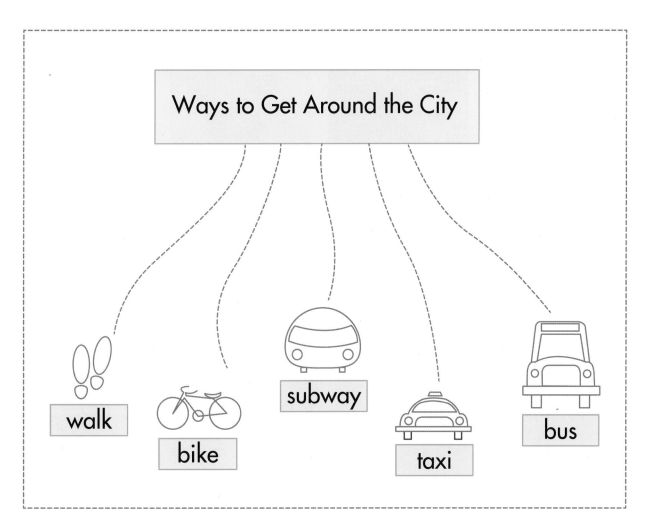

Ways to Get Around the City

walk

bike

subway

taxi

bus

Words to Know

bike   bus   subway   taxi

Index